THE INDOOR GARDENER

CREATIVE DESIGNS FOR PLANTS IN THE HOME, WITH 120 INSPIRATIONAL PICTURES

DIANA YAKELEY

WITH PHOTOGRAPHY BY CAROLINE ARBER

LORENZ BOOKS

This edition is published by Lorenz Books,
an imprint of Anness Publishing Ltd,
Hermes House,
88–89 Blackfriars Road,
London SE1 8HA
tel. 020 7401 2077; fax 020 7633 9499

www.lorenzbooks.com; www.annesspublishing.com

If you like the images in this book and would
like to investigate using them for publishing,
promotions or advertising, please visit our website
www.practicalpictures.com for more information.

UK agent: The Manning Partnership Ltd
tel. 01225 478444; fax 01225 478440
sales@manning-partnership.co.uk

UK distributor: Book Trade Services; tel. 0116 2759086;
fax 0116 2759090; uksales@booktradeservices.com;
exportsales@booktradeservices.com

North American agent/distributor:
National Book Network
tel. 301 459 3366; fax 301 429 5746;
www.nbnbooks.com

Australian agent/distributor: Pan Macmillan Australia
tel. 1300 135 113; fax 1300 135 103;
customer.service@macmillan.com.au

New Zealand agent/distributor:
David Bateman Ltd
tel. (09) 415 7664; fax (09) 415 8892

Publisher Joanna Lorenz
Senior Editor Lucy Doncaster
Designer Lucy Doncaster
Photographer Caroline Arber
Stylist Charlotte Melling
Production Controller Mai Ling Collyer

ETHICAL TRADING POLICY
Because of our ongoing ecological investment programme,
you, as our customer, can have the pleasure and reassurance
of knowing that a tree is being cultivated on your behalf
to naturally replace the materials used to make the book
you are holding. For further information about this
scheme, go to www.annesspublishing.com/trees

Previously published as part of a larger volume,
Indoor Gardening

PUBLISHER'S NOTE
Although the advice and information in this book are
believed to be accurate and true at the time of going to
press, neither the authors nor the publisher can accept
any legal responsibility or liability for any errors or
omissions that may be made nor for any inaccuracies
nor for any harm or injury that comes about from
following instructions or advice in this book.

contents

introduction

As a small child I spent my pocket money on buying tiny plants and lined them up on my windowsill. They gave me great pleasure, impressed my parents and taught me about nature and nurture, responsibility and failure, and apparently cleaned the air in my bedroom at the same time. I sold the duplicates and offsets at the garden gate, which taught me the rudiments of commerce. What I did not consider at the time was the element of design needed to put the plants into a context, a place where they not only flourished, but formed part of a designed interior, too. Too much perhaps for a six-year-old.

The need to reaffirm our link with nature and to be surrounded with living plants is fundamental. The more we communicate through virtual reality and electronic data, the greater our need to touch base with real organic matter.

The synergy between horticulture and street culture is evident through the number of style magazines that are aimed at a generation who are not traditionally interested in gardening and plants. Fashion now spills over into most aspects of design and there are new ways to combine clothes, homes and gardens. Handling plants seems to be a basic human desire and most rooms, however minimal, come alive with flowers and leaves to enhance them.

Today, there are numerous books on interiors and gardening, but there are few that combine the two, and that is what I hope to address in this book. Choosing the right container and position for your houseplant can elevate it to a piece of living sculpture, a work of art that draws the eye and complements the colours and textures of your home.

Below The delicate leaves of ruby chard seedlings (*Beta vulgaris*) look perfect on a sunny kitchen window ledge.

Below Trailing ivy (*Hedera helix*) is happy to grow in low light levels and a moist atmosphere – perfect for a bathroom.

Above The addition of colourful plants, such as the bead plant (*Nertera granadensis*), helps enliven any space, including an office.

Above The architectural purity of this stairway is complemented by mounds of mind-your-own-business (*Soleirolia soleirolii*).

Successfully combining the plant, container and interior, as well as enhancing the colour scheme, is the art of indoor gardening. The mood and style of a room can be dramatically altered by the addition of a lush, vibrantly coloured plant or a large, dramatic architectural specimen. My own philosophy is to keep things simple. The contemporary interior is about space, light and reduction, with less clutter and larger areas of glass making it the perfect setting for well-chosen plants. Only specimen plants with sculptural lines will look right here, whereas a traditional interior will happily absorb prettier, more rounded plants. We have included a range of ideas for different looks and locations around the house, so there is something for everyone.

In the past, people treated the indoor plant as something that should go on forever and felt that to admit defeat with an ageing spider plant was tantamount to poisoning your granny. Many indoor plants have been forced in greenhouses and imported under unnatural conditions,

and so will not last forever in a house. But growing indoor plants is always better value than buying cut flowers, and when they are past their best either try propagating from them, recycle or compost them, or throw them away.

Nothing is more depressing than an unhealthy indoor plant. For this reason, discipline is important when shopping for plants. Impulse buys at garden centres should be avoided until you have worked out exactly where you wish to place the latest acquisition. An unsuitable position may be all right for a short time, but sooner or later it will take its toll. Given the right conditions, as well as proper care and attention, however, most indoor plants will flourish, and our section on plant care will help you keep your plants in top condition.

For me, plants have become an obsession and a therapy. Concentrating on these little miracles of nature will take your mind off the strains of modern living, provide visual delight, and enhance your environment at the same time. Quite a return on a relatively small investment.

design points

In an age where the prefix 'designer' applies to almost everything, the indoor plant has somehow missed out. The successful combination of plant, pot and context rarely happens. With a little thought, all this can change.

Left Plant and ornaments marry well here, with the rounded bowls echoing the pleasing shape of this hybrid *Begonia* 'Norah Bedson'.

scale and proportion

Designers draw plans to show how each part of a design will work, taking into account the space, light levels and function of the area. This is too much like hard work for indoor planting, but the same principles apply. Careful thought about size and position will create balance in an interior.

First of all, stand back and look at your rooms, then ask yourself the following questions. Are the ceilings high or low? How much light comes into the room and when? Are there areas that need hiding or emphasizing? Once you have decided on these points, look at the proportions of the space and consider whether a big statement plant or a group of plants with a similar theme would look better.

Be bold with size and shape. The reason most indoor plants seem insignificant is because they are too small, overwhelmed by large furniture and high ceilings. Big and bold plants need space for their sculptural quality and architectural form to be fully appreciated. Remember that you will not be able to move large containers around often, so ensure that the plants have enough light from the start.

Large plants look best in contemporary, open-plan areas where the furniture has clean, spare lines and there is ample circulation space around the plant. Groups of similar pots with blocks of planting can also achieve this look. Small, charming arrangements work well in more intimate spaces. They also look wonderful if displayed in multiples to form a miniature indoor landscape. Rows of bamboo stems, sprouting acorns or avocado stones (pits) in glass containers are much more interesting than just one.

Very large containers sometimes look best planted with low-growing, geometric plants, with the pot being the dominant feature. In contrast, smaller plants can spill over the edges of their containers, the interest focusing on the plant. As a rough guide, a two-thirds/one-third proportion works well. With a large pot, the one-third should be the planting, the two-thirds the container, while with smaller containers, two-thirds should be the planting and one-third the container. Rules are there to be broken, however, and, with a little practice, scale and proportion can be manipulated to great effect. Tiny plants grouped together en masse become a grand statement, while one large plant can look so perfectly proportioned in its space that it blends seamlessly with the interior.

Opposite These spectacular banana plants (*Musa*) help to create a smooth transition between the interior and the patio. The large, metallic pots subtly echo the metal floor grilles and door frames.
Left Groups of objects can create an interesting arrangement. Green bamboo shoots, rooted in water in miniature vases and displayed inside tall glass holders, are arranged with spiky fruits.

style and placement

Most rooms tell a unique story about the lives of their owners: cool, modern, international jet-setter; eclectic foreign traveller; young urban professional; or comfortable country-dweller. Developing a design statement extends not only to the choice of furnishings and furniture, but also to the type of indoor plants. The designer's skill is then in selecting plants and pots that emphasize and complement the interior design and materials of the room, and so continue this personal theme.

Carefully study the room in question and decide whether it is formal or informal, classic or contemporary, rustic or urban chic, and then gauge whether the plant and container are in keeping with the style. If they are not, then the arrangement will never look right. For example, a sophisticated, white, minimal room needs nothing more than, say, a perfect white orchid in a precise glass container to emphasize the reduction of ornament and the purity of the space, whereas a country kitchen is a great place for a profusion of herbs in old terracotta pots. Both arrangements reflect the spirit of the room and reinforce the aesthetic of the interior design.

Once you have established the 'look' you are trying to achieve, the question of positioning and grouping the containers becomes all-important. If there is a fireplace, it will form a natural focal point in the room and the mantelpiece is the ideal place for displaying a group of plants when the fire is not in use. If the fireplace is a long way from the window, then move the plants to a sunnier spot, or outside, for part of the time to recuperate.

Bookshelves, ledges and alcoves can all be beautifully enhanced with indoor plants, but it is perhaps the coffee table that can create the most impact, becoming the centre of attention with a crisp, low-level collection of plants and books. A grid arrangement of square containers planted with identical plants might look good here, as would a long low trough running the length of the table.

In general, plants look best grouped in odd numbers, that is in threes, fives and so on, but this is not a hard-and-fast rule. Indeed, a grid of even numbers that forms a single feature works brilliantly and creates the impression of a miniature indoor garden. Add objects with a similar shape or colour to the grouping in order to create a story about texture or form, or add a single cut bloom of the same hue or complexity.

Above These delicate golden bamboos (*Phyllostachys aurea*) form a gentle living screen from the street, without blocking out the light. They could also be placed outdoors during the summer.

Opposite A brightly lit alcove is the perfect spot for sun-loving purple basil (*Ocimum basilicum* 'Purple Ruffles'). Although plants usually look best in odd numbers, using two pots and combining them with a group of simple vases is just right.

form and shape

Many of the plants included in this book have been chosen for their simple geometric form, their pared-down structure and the sense of balance they bring to a group of objects in a room. Strong form and shape is important in the modern, streamlined home.

Many of today's homes contain less clutter than ever before and allow more light to flood in. The popularity of white walls, wood or stone floors, as well as a few carefully chosen pieces of furniture, is in tune with the celebrated German architect Mies van der Rohe's statement of the 1950s that "less is more". However, simply reducing the number of objects in an interior is not enough. Each piece in the room, including the indoor plants, must not only be of great beauty in its own right, but should complement the other pieces around it in order to form a harmonious whole.

A single flower or leaf in a vase can often have more impact than a whole bunch, allowing the eye to contemplate and appreciate the shape of the plant more easily. The importance of form also applies to the choice of indoor plants. A group of identical plants arranged together in order to create one geometric shape, such as a row of mind-your-own-business (*Soleirolia soleirolii*), may be chosen to echo another design element in the room and so strengthen the overall visual impact.

Getting the design right involves meticulous attention to detail, so that the end result looks effortlessly right. Rather than having a collection of mismatched plants and pots scattered haphazardly around the house, sit down and examine why they don't look as good as they could. It may be that the shape, character or colour of the plant bears no relation to the container or to the objects close by, let alone to the style of the home. For this reason, the arrangement will never sit easily in the room. Try taking everything off a shelf or windowsill and replacing all the objects with one perfect orchid or a starkly simple glass or Perspex (Plexiglas) container planted with a row of lustrous *Iris reticulata*. Then, just stand back and assess whether this treatment suits the space.

Opposite The natural shape of these mind-your-own-business (*Soleirolia soleirolii*) suggests an indoor topiary display. The softly tactile foliage perfectly balances the severity of the fire surround.
Left A Perspex (Plexiglas) container on a glass shelf provides a wonderful showcase for the intense colour and complex form of these starkly beautiful *Iris reticulata*.

colour and scent

Two of the best attributes that plants can bring to almost any interior are colour and scent. A burst of vivid colour in a neutral design scheme can change the whole balance of the room and create a real focal point. Match it with a hue or highlight in a painting or a cushion, and create a subtly co-ordinated look.

We talk of colour in terms of temperature – red and yellow are warm, blue and green are cool. Different colours are also linked with different moods and emotions. White is calming, purifying and contemplative, while the fiery orange of, say, a bird-of-paradise (*Strelitzia reginae*) suggests South American heat and a fiery temperament. Think of the emotional impact of newly emerging crocuses after the grey of winter, the intimation of sunshine of those first spring daffodils and the spiritual uplift a fresh sharp green brings after a dusty day in the city.

If you wish to create a harmonious design scheme, choose plants that have similar hues to your furnishings. To bring a touch of excitement and drama to a design, choose a plant with a strongly contrasting colour. The bright red *Guzmania lingulata*, for example, looks stunning against a deep purple or blue wall.

You can also use a combination of cut flowers and foliage plants to create different colour effects. For example, the purple-splashed foliage of *Gynura sarmentosa* looks intriguing next to the purplish-red and pink tones of a bunch of sweet peas. The number of beautiful combinations you can create is endless once your eye is trained to see similarities of colour or texture. With the right pot, the end result can be a perfect still life and very pleasing to the eye.

The seasons also have their colour associations. Spring brings the freshness of white, blue or pink hyacinths and lemon-yellow daffodils, as well as the soft acid green of new growth. Summer makes us think of hot pink bougainvillea and scarlet pelargoniums which, in turn, lead to the more muted shades of autumn and winter. Plants from all over the world are now available locally, and you can buy all kinds of exotica at any time of the year. It is, though, more pleasurable to work with the seasons.

Left The delicate white or coloured flowers of the popular *Hyacinthus orientalis* have a powerful, delightful scent and make a stunning addition to any room.

Above Try to suit the colour of a plant to its location. Here, the fiery red bracts of tropical *Guzmania lingulata* look stunning against a deep blue wall.

Above The sinuous organic form of a beautiful white moth orchid (*Phalaenopsis*) contrasts strikingly with the severe lines of this colourful piece of modern art.

The scent of flowers and foliage is an added bonus at any time of the year and can evoke powerful memories of childhood or special people, places and events. With the huge variety of plants now available from most garden centres and markets, it is possible to have year-round colour and scent from indoor plants such as paper-white narcissi (*Narcissus papyraceus*), *Gardenia augusta*, jasmine (*Jasminum polyanthum*), *Stephanotis floribunda*, cherry pie (*Heliotropium arborescens*) and hyacinths (*Hyacinthus* spp.).

As well as the many delightfully scented flowering plants on offer, there is also a host of herbs that have the most evocative of perfumes, and which thrive indoors.

The fresh scent of mint (*Mentha*) and the warm Mediterranean bouquet of rosemary (*Rosmarinus*) add to the delicious aromas of a kitchen, while lavender has a powerful sleep-inducing fragrance, as well as wonderful mauve flowerheads and silvery grey foliage. Pots of basil, with their fresh green leaves and pungent aroma, seem a natural addition to any kitchen, no matter how small.

Most herbs need high light levels and so a sunny kitchen windowsill is the best place to grow them. Some require more water than others, and you should check them regularly to ensure they don't rot in potentially steamy conditions.

texture and pattern

Plants, particularly foliage plants, can add a richness of texture and pattern to the overall design of a room. The glorious intricacy of some leaves, stems and tendrils is a natural foil to the limited palette of colours and range of materials that is often found in the modern interior.

Many of the best houseplants are grown for their magnificent leaves, which often look like landscapes in their own right. Deep fissures and grooves, spots and veins, pleats and puckers, hairs and sticky bits, all add to the complex fascination of the plant. The gently ribbed leaves of a banana plant (*Musa*) instantly bring a tropical ambience to a living room, while the amazing fan-like pleats of the coconut palm (*Cocos nucifera*) or the delicate tracery of a miniature bamboo conjure up images of the Far East. Interesting textures invite you to reach out and touch them. It is hard to resist patting the wonderful mounds of *Soleirolia soleirolii*, the mind-your-own-business plant, while the translucent beauty of *Sparrmannia africana* when light shines through its pale, downy leaves is breathtaking.

Succulents, with their amazing ability to store moisture, display particularly varied textures and patterns. The elegant, magisterial *Aeonium* 'Zwartkop' has smooth, shiny black rosettes, while the echeverias have soft, matt, greeny blue foliage that looks wonderfully modern in a metal container (although their petal-like delicacy would look equally at home in a traditional interior). Members of the large *Kalanchoe* genus provide colour, form and texture, and positively thrive on neglect. The fleshy leaves are often tipped with subtle colour, particularly *K. thyrsiflora*, whose

pale green leaves are tinged with red and covered in a soft bloom. But, of the succulents, perhaps the ultimate in minimalism are the living stones (*Lithops*). With their pairs of fat, fleshy leaves, which part to allow through a flower, they have a science-fiction air about them.

Even the simple addition of a mulch or top-dressing can give an arrangement added texture, setting off the plant to perfection, while also helping to retain moisture. Indeed, some of the more subtle plants look better displayed against a background of white gravel or crushed shell. A layer of sand beneath a cactus suggests a mini desert, while seashells are reminiscent of summer at the beach. Paying attention to the finishing touches in this way will ensure your displays look well designed.

We are all familiar with the irregular patterning of begonia and pelargonium leaves, but for a truly weird experience, look to carnivorous plants, such as pitcher plants (*Sarracenia*) and Venus flytraps (*Dionaea muscipula*), for their intricate form, grasping little claws or juicy pitcher-shaped flytraps. They need either rainwater or filtered, lime-free tap water as heavily chlorinated water will kill them. The markings on pitcher plants are strangely beautiful and often richly variegated. They live on flying insects and are the most eco-friendly way of keeping flying pests at bay.

Opposite The geometric precision of this display is echoed in the mathematical complexity of the succulents, although their rosette-like structure brings some softness to the grid.

Right Blue-grey slate top-dresses this zinc container to create a crunchy contrast with the smooth, lush greenery of a banana (*Musa*).

interior ideas

Plants enhance every part of the house, but, in terms of ideal growing conditions, some rooms will present a challenge. With flair and a little know-how, however, even the darkest hallway or bathroom can play host to some greenery.

Left Indoor plants come into their own in winter. Here, a linear arrangement of objects and plants brings a stark mantelshelf to life.

living rooms

Living rooms tend to be warmer and drier than other rooms, and often have a greater ratio of windows to floor area. This is ideal for some houseplants, but not for those that need a cooler site, so care needs to be taken with plant choice. Damp-loving plants need not apply.

The living room is quite often the room in the house on which you spend the most money and thought, so it is important to choose the right plants to complete the picture. Well-chosen species can lead the eye to a particular piece of furniture or group of objects, co-ordinating the colours or textures. Play shapes and colours off against one another for further interest or add height with a large specimen plant to a corner of a room in which most of the furniture is at a fairly uniformly low level.

Many homes have rooms that combine dining, cooking and relaxing in one open-plan space. In such an area, bold architectural plants would go well with the strong, clean lines of modern furniture. It is better to spend more on one or two truly wonderful mature specimen plants with a good shape and habit than to have a number of smaller plants dotted around the house. A single specimen can look dramatic or two specimens can be used, placed either side of a doorway – perhaps one leading outside. Large single specimen plants can also look impressive silhouetted against a window. Take care when the temperature outside falls too low, however, because few plants can take both heat and extremes of cold and draught, and you may need to move them away from the window. Frequent misting is advisable if the room is hot and dry.

Opposite Sprouted wheatgrass (*Elymus*) makes for an unexpectedly sophisticated arrangement in the right container. White stones are used to disguise the compost. The linear and precise design of both the table and sofa are mirrored in the clipped cushions of wheatgrass and white stones.

The choice of plants for a living room should be guided by the decor. The powerful verdancy of the tray of wheatgrass (*Elymus*) and white stones shown here reflects the style of the room and provides a focal point in an otherwise neutral, white interior, but, perhaps most important of all, it does not impede circulation around the table. Indeed, with heavily trafficked areas, it is better to have plants that do not intrude into the space too much as they will be constantly bruised and battered. Juiced, wheatgrass is said to be a great cure for hangovers and research is ongoing into its other curative properties. Kept clipped and watered, it will keep fresh for several weeks before it needs replacing with freshly sprouted wheat grains.

In a more traditional, less open-plan home, the living room may also be the most formal room in the house – a quiet spot for reading or a place for entertaining. This calls for more elegant arrangements, such as roses or lilies planted in geometric containers or smaller, neat glass or ceramic pots filled with seasonal bulbs positioned on either side of sofas. In spring, these could be irises and tulips, while in autumn and winter the shapely cyclamen flowers come into their own.

For many people the living area is used only at night after a day's work and, during the autumn and winter, it is also often only seen in artificial light. If you have adjustable downlights, try tilting one to highlight a particular plant and, for further dramatic effect, dim the lights elsewhere. Lighting the plant from below a glass table can also be very effective and is especially good if the container is interesting or is made from a reflective material.

dining rooms

The concept of having a separate room for dining is fast becoming a thing of the past. Often, the dining room has to double up as a work room or office. However, it is difficult to resist the urge to place a few plants in such a large area, and they can be decorative additions to festive meals.

Indoor plant displays for the dining room may be formal or informal. A display of gardenias, with their compact shape, glossy leaves and wonderful fragrance, is a particularly good choice for a formal dining-table arrangement. Planted in polished aluminium pots, they look very smart, matching the gleaming silverware and newly starched white linen. The result is simple, elegant and fresh, while also leaving enough space to accommodate a plethora of serving dishes and flickering candles for a celebration dinner.

Pleasing and evocative effects can also be produced by decorating the table with spotlessly clean pots of edible plants in order to forge a link with the food. Mat-forming Corsican mint (*Mentha requienii*), for example, makes a pungent dining-table decoration, while very small bay, citrus or rosemary plants suggest Mediterranean meals under the sun. Although strictly a garden plant, rosemary (*Rosmarinus officinalis*) is a highly aromatic evergreen herb that makes an attractive occasional visitor indoors. Some suppliers sell miniature fruiting olive

trees in old terracotta pots. These too would look wonderful marching down the centre of an old pine table for a relaxed Sunday lunch with friends and family, conjuring up memories of shared trips abroad and good, simple food.

In general, planting should be kept to a low level so that it doesn't obscure your vision across the table. A low-level plant at each place setting can be both charming and practical. Herbs such as thyme, with their compact habit and delicious smells and tastes, are ideal candidates for this treatment. Other small, clump-forming plants, such as mind-your-own-business (*Soleirolia soleirolii*), with its delicate froth of tiny leaves, or the bright orange bead plant (*Nertera granadensis*), would be just as suitable, although the latter two are not edible. Even cress and mustard, grown in tiny eggcups or tea-light holders, can be charming and humorous.

Plants on dining tables should obviously be kept in pristine condition, and you don't really want to be looking at potting compost (soil mix) while eating or entertaining. An excellent idea for embellishing a dining-table display is to use small fruits or nuts as a decorative mulch. For example, kumquats look brilliant placed under sprouting spring bulbs. In autumn and winter, you might like to try using dried kidney beans, lentils or walnuts in their shells. Organic top dressings should be removed before they begin to rot.

Left For a seasonally themed dinner party, arrange small terracotta flowerpots planted with club moss (*Selaginella*) and thyme along the table. Use seed labels written with felt-tipped pens for the place names.

Below A simple, silver-and-white theme is perfect for a celebratory meal. The low-level plant arrangements do not obstruct the view across the table, while *Gardenia augusta* 'Veitchiana' **(top left)** adds a delicious scent to the air. Just before the meal, tie fresh gardenia leaves to white napkins with knotted blades of grass **(top right)**. The dark green leaves of the gardenias are the perfect foil for the rose-like white flowers.

kitchens

Every gardener will want to include plants in the kitchen. The preparation and presentation of food are enhanced by the addition of a few fresh leaves, so a selection of herbs on the windowsill is an obvious choice. However, there are also decorative indoor plants that will add interest to the kitchen.

It is difficult to resist having some indoor plants on your kitchen windowsill, whether they are edible plants, such as herbs and salad leaves, or purely decorative. It just seems to be the right place for sprouting pips and seeds, rooting some broken-off sedum leaves or growing some fiery chilli peppers. Kitchens are warm and steamy, and you can observe the progress (or lack of it) of your plants while doing some other task.

The ease of snipping the youngest, most succulent, mixed salad leaves from a window box and throwing them into a salad bowl in six seconds takes some beating. If you grow cut-and-come-again varieties, you can just cut what you need, rather than harvesting a whole lettuce, and you can also sow more seed as spaces appear in the container. In this way, you will have a constant supply of fresh salad leaves that you have grown yourself. You can buy packets of mixed seed from many suppliers so that you can have a good selection of different leaves for a summer salad.

Another attractive alternative to a window box of salad leaves would be to grow some ruby or rhubarb chard (*Beta vulgaris*) on a kitchen window ledge. Grown in an old terracotta pot, it would look spectacular with the light shining through the leaves.

Opposite All the accessories in this kitchen come together to enhance the homely, rustic atmosphere. Sunshine streams through salad leaves and the cut stems of clover are perfectly placed in an enamel jug.
Right Using kitchen containers for edible plants is a gentle visual pun. Rhubarb can be grown indoors in a large container for a short time, but should then be planted in the garden.

A useful addition to an ever-expanding windowsill is the elegant *Aloe vera*. With its stark sculptural shape, it is reminiscent of the desert and is possibly the only plant suitable for the most minimal of kitchens. Aloe vera gel, which is extracted from the leaf, can be applied externally to promote the healing of cuts, burns, sunburn, eczema and skin irritation, to name just a few of its wonderful medicinal properties. In the commercial production of aloe vera gel, the leaves are cut and the sap is used fresh, preserved and bottled or dried to a brown crystalline solid for use in creams, lotions and medicinal preparations. In the home, you can rub the sap on to those inevitable agave lacerations and painful cactus punctures in the skin on your hands.

bedrooms

Although many modern bedrooms have built-in storage and contain little else but a bed and a bedside table, you should not let this restrict your choice of indoor plants. If space is a problem, then the most practical choice is an interesting selection of small, compact plant arrangements.

Pots of sprouting spring bulbs are fresh and spare, and have the added advantage of producing a delicious scent, while simple bowls of white or cream miniature roses would be perfect in an all-white bedroom, sensuous and pure at the same time. Complete the design with the finest crisp, white bed linen and armfuls of scented, white cut flowers.

Orchids, such as moth orchids (*Phalaenopsis*) and slipper orchids (*Paphiopedilum*), look just right in a bedroom. They

come in a variety of different colours, which you can harmonize with the colour scheme of your room. You could place a white orchid, for example, near some black-and-white photographs of flowers, allowing the graphic quality of both to create a wonderfully strong combination.

Lavender has sleep-inducing properties, as well as being a pleasing colour for a bedroom. It needs warm sunlight, though, so it is best saved for a short visit to the bedroom before going back to the garden.

Cut some flowerheads to put under your pillow for a serene night's sleep. Similarly, the soft blue of a Cape leadwort (*Plumbago auriculata*) would look stunning in a bedroom window or climbing in from a sheltered balcony, but it really needs a conservatory (sun room) and so is best just brought into a guest bedroom for a few days.

Bedrooms that have lots of surfaces, such as chests of drawers, dressing tables or even perhaps a little table next to a comfortable chair for reading, are ideal for a few indoor plants. Link the colour of the flowers to the colour of the soft furnishings. Be bold and create a sense of theatre with an ornate and decadent antique bed matched with the mysterious, nocturnal-looking flowerhead of the devil flower (*Tacca chantrieri*).

A softly curved container planted with a pretty flowering plant would work well in a bedroom, whether you choose the delicate beauty of an iris or cyclamen, the frilly flowers of eustoma or the bolder velvety delights of a bowl of pansies (*Viola*). Choose from the drama of the near-black *V.* 'Molly Sanderson' or the intense blue of some of the other varieties, or just a wonderful patchwork of colour from a packet of mixed seeds. Pansies are available in a variety of colours, so opt for a single hue or a mixture of different shades for a more riotous effect, depending on the style and colour of the decor and soft furnishings in the room.

Left A brightly coloured *Campanula isophylla* in a curvaceous pot is top-dressed with tiny mother-of-pearl buttons here. It looks ultra-feminine in this all-white bedroom.

Top left The amethyst colours of these lovely hellebores (*Helleborus*) tone perfectly with the bedcovers and cushions in a comfortable bedroom. Hellebores are, strictly speaking, garden plants, enjoying cold conditions, but they can be brought indoors for a few days to decorate a guest bedroom.

Top right A flower-strewn, satin- and silk-upholstered French bed, combined with a curvy, flesh-pink pot, creates an air of decadence. The truly exotic bat or devil flower (*Tacca chantrieri*) has something of the night about it too.

Left The contrasting textures of suede and leather, fur and linen in neutral colours make for a tactile and sensuous bedroom, further enhanced by this orchid, *Paphiopedilum parishii*.

bathrooms

Bathrooms are for unwinding. Imagine candles, a glass of chilled wine, a scented bath oil and luxuriously soft, fluffy towels for the ultimate bathing experience – soothing, sensual and relaxing after a day in a grey city. Lush greenery is the obvious choice for these watery havens.

For most people, splashing around in water is an invigorating or calming pastime, as well as a refreshing necessity. Many plants enjoy the same watery pleasures, and what could be better than some organic greenery on a bathroom shelf or windowsill?

Plants with a good form and shape are ideal for a bathroom. Miniature bamboos look crisp, clean and contemporary in a row of identical containers. These bamboos love to be damp, and look suitably Zen-like in a modern bathroom, especially if a container can be found that suggests the Far East or relates in some way to the materials used in the bathroom.

Ferns and aquatic plants enjoy the damp air in a bathroom. Ferns are happy in fairly low light levels and most love to be damp and misted, their delicate fronds making a perfect foil to a tiled room. There are a huge number of varieties to choose from, including the glossy-leaved aspleniums and the hard fern (*Blechnum gibbum*) with its uncurling fronds. Aquatic plants, such as the umbrella plant (*Cyperus involucratus*), need their feet in water at all times, and are quite happy in the corner of a bathroom. The stems are easily bent, so snip off any offending tufts.

Above Enjoying a soak, these hard ferns (*Blechnum gibbum*) look just right with Victorian taps and an old-fashioned sink.

Left The umbrella plant (*Cyperus involucratus*) is happy in this moist bathroom. It is set off beautifully by the green walls. Needing to have its feet in water, a bathroom is the perfect room for growing this plant.

hallways

Most hallways are relatively dark, narrow and draughty, with a radiator – not the ideal place for growing indoor plants. However, this is also the room where first impressions are made, so do keep some plants here, but choose types that will thrive in less than perfect conditions.

To enhance the less than showy plants that will survive in a dark hallway, use interesting or colourful containers. Where the container is the main interest in terms of shape and form, the plant can play a less important role. You will also need to make sure that the containers are not too unsteady, however, as this is an area where coats are removed and umbrellas shaken.

If you want brightly coloured flowering plants, you may have to accept that, after a few weeks, they will have to be moved to a more suitable situation or back into the garden. Rooted plants are better value than cut flowers in terms of longevity, but may have been forced in unnatural conditions and so will not last forever, no matter how hard you try.

The plants you can grow in the hallway will obviously depend on how much space there is. If you are fortunate enough to have a large hall, with top light from windows around the staircase, grow large architectural specimens that can use the height of the stairwell to great advantage, growing up between the floors. If your hallway is rather small, make use of the stairs themselves. A row of plants marching up the stairs is fun, but choose compact types such as the soft plump mounds of mind-your-own-business (*Soleirolia soleirolii*) or club moss (*Selaginella*).

The hallway is also a link with the outside and, sometimes, small specimen trees such as privet (*Ligustrum*) can be moved from the doorstep for brief periods of time. During periods of intense cold, outdoor plants can also overwinter here, but make sure that the heat does not dry out the roots.

Below The indoor-outdoor look is perfect for the transitional space between a living area and the outside in a large hallway. Privet (*Ligustrum*) standards in smart zinc planters look equally at home on the outside porch framing the front door or in the hallway. This is a good place to overwinter the plants in cold weather.

planting schemes

Whether your preferences tend
to bold architectural plants,
brightly coloured arrangements
or more subtle, spare schemes,
there are plenty of simple ways to
arrange indoor plants so they are
displayed to their best effect,
whatever the season.

Left These pale lavender *Primula obconica* are given a
contemporary twist by being planted in grass baskets.

architectural plants

If plants are to make a positive addition to an interior, they should be compatible with the space in terms of size and shape. Plants with a strong form and shape can make a dramatic impact on a room, becoming a piece of sculpture in their own right.

Modern architecture creates free-flowing spaces with large expanses of light, reducing unnecessary elements and inducing a sense of calm. The plants that are most suited to this type of space are those whose strong form and leaf structure are the main interest, rather than an intricate flower. The pot, too, must have strong, simple lines to complement the plant and the surrounding architecture.

A large specimen bush that looks wonderful in a room with a high ceiling and plenty of light is the African hemp (*Sparrmannia africana*). It is perfect for standing on a table to give a vertical element to a room. The huge downy

leaves look ethereal with light shining behind them, while the lime-green colour looks fresh throughout the year. Always water with rainwater, or at least not with hard water, to avoid brown blotches.

The Canary date palm (*Phoenix canariensis*), a classic indoor plant that will flourish if it has plenty of light, has elegant, arching fronds that create a striking focal point in a large, plain white container. Another architectural group of plants, *Dracaena*, contains many species of palm-like plants from Africa and Asia. They create the impression of an exotic plant, while actually being quite tough. This has made them very popular indoor plants. Dracaenas rely on simple but very striking variegation and a bold outline for their attraction. *D. marginata* 'Tricolor' is particularly striking, with green, cream and red striped leaves.

The sculptural beauty of the *Agave* genus also bears closer inspection. The fleshy leaves unfold from a central core and are so closely packed that they leave an indentation on the next leaf and create a pattern of mathematical intricacy. *A. americana* has beautiful blue-grey colouring, although the dull green *A. victoriae-reginae* is more reliable indoors.

Some members of the fig (*Ficus*) genus make excellent indoor plants and come in different forms. The weeping fig (*Ficus benjamina*) can grow to a great height given the right conditions. Another species of fig, the creeping fig

Left Light pouring through the soft green leaves of African hemp (*Sparrmannia africana*) reveals the delicate tracery of veins and shows off the structural form very well.

Above Though a young specimen, this common fig (*Ficus carica*) has the form of an old gnarled tree. The antique terracotta pot also suggests age and the passing of many seasons.

Above The graceful tree fern *Dicksonia fibrosa* needs a large space for its scale and character to be fully appreciated. It needs to be kept moist and the trunk should be sprayed on a regular basis.

(*F. pumila*), is a small spreading version that will happily grow at the base of its larger relative. They both respond well to generous feeding. Some specimens of fig are grown for their sculptural beauty. *F. carica*, for example, has clean lines and well-defined branches, the shape of which can be maintained by careful clipping and pruning.

Bamboos can be grown indoors where there are high light levels, although they will benefit from being outside for some of the time. Their strong vertical canes contrast with the delicacy of their leaves, making them ideal candidates for the architectural category. They have a Zen-like quality, and make a perfect translucent screen for windows or to delineate spaces.

Over recent years, many garden centres have been selling strange, hairy logs that, according to the instructions, will produce exotic shoots from the crown if they are planted in potting compost (soil mix) and watered well. These are the magnificent tree ferns, which originate mainly from New Zealand and Australian rainforests. The cut-log variety is usually *Dicksonia antarctica*, which will do well in a cool conservatory (sun room), provided the trunk is watered almost daily for six months until roots have formed at the base and the spectacular fronds appear from the crown. *D. fibrosa* is usually sold already rooted by specialist nurseries, but also requires a cool, light spot and needs its trunk to be misted.

bold and brilliant

We all have preferences when it comes to the colours we use in the design of our interiors. The colours of our indoor plants, as well as those of the walls, floors and soft furnishings, can also be used as an expression of our own unique personal style.

Most people use colours from the paler end of the spectrum to paint their homes because light reflects off pale colours and makes walls visually recede, thus giving a feeling of spaciousness. In contrast, darker colours advance, making the room seem smaller and more intimate. However, dark colours are useful in certain situations. Not only do they disguise blemishes, but they also make pictures and objects seen against them stand out more clearly. This is advisable for older or larger houses with high ceilings and less than perfect walls.

In the same way, the use of boldly colourful plants can transform a room and create a focal point. A tiny splash of intense colour can lift a room from being rather ordinary to something highly creative. Think of purple irises in a yellow room, bright orange marigolds or sunflowers in a pale grey one, or the pink, paddle-shaped bracts of *Tillandsia cyanea*

teamed with toning towels in an all-white bathroom.

One of the most spectacular, and unusually coloured, plants is *Aeonium* 'Zwartkop', a succulent with fleshy, dark reddish-black rosettes held on branches off a main stem. It likes to be kept cool in winter and needs bright light in spring and summer when its leaves will darken with the light. Not many plants are black, so this is a wonderful piece of plant sculpture.

Certain flower colours are seasonal: yellow and blue in spring, pinks, reds and oranges in summer, and more muted oranges and golds in autumn. With plants being flown in from all over the world, this is not a hard-and-fast rule to follow, but it is rewarding to acknowledge the seasons and work with them. Indeed, one of the great joys of spring is to see new green shoots emerging from bulbs and the promise of sunshine in a trough of yellow daffodils.

Some plants with bright summer colours, such as bougainvilleas and mandevilleas, are best grown in a conservatory (sun room). If you do not have a conservatory, there are other brightly flowered plants that can be grown indoors, such as hybrids of *Kalanchoe blossfeldiana*. These have small, leathery, serrated leaves that often turn reddish in strong sunlight. They produce clusters of long-lasting, small flowers in shades of red, orange, yellow and lilac. Although naturally spring-flowering, commercial growers are able to produce flowering specimens throughout the year.

Chilli peppers (*Capsicum annuum* Longum Group) can be relied on to make bright, shiny splashes of colour in the autumn, ranging from lipstick-red to polished deep purple to green. Their compact bushiness makes them suitable as a centrepiece on a dining or kitchen table in very simple containers. They are raw and earthy, rather like baked earth, a reminder of hot summers, as well as being invaluable for cooking.

Left Very few plants are as near black as the architectural succulent *Aeonium* 'Zwartkop'. The contrast between the white pot and the dark rosette-like foliage is bold and striking.

Above A neatly arranged row of
ornamental hot chilli peppers
(*Capsicum annuum* Longum Group)
make for a bold display on a
mantelpiece. The flame-shaped fruits
above a fireplace are very apt.

Right The odd little bead plant
(*Nertera granadensis*) has clusters
of vibrant little orange berries, which
make a wonderful contrast to muted
greys, creams and whites.

Far right These striking, bright
yellow *Narcissus* 'Tête-à-Tête' boldly
announce the arrival of spring.

pale and pure

Softer pale colours are relaxing, subtle and unthreatening. They can be used in a bedroom to create a soothing atmosphere or in an informal living room or dining area where you can rest, unwind and recuperate from the stresses of the day.

For those who find the brilliant white of many modern paints too cold or bland, there are hundreds of whites with the merest hint of pale colour that give a more relaxed feel to walls. Try putting a brighter flower in the same hue against these to bring out the subtlety of colour – it may be all you need to bring the colour alive. Pale walls will also emphasize the shape of the plants, throwing them into stark relief, as well as reflecting light around them.

Pale colours remind us of faded fabrics. The traditional toile de Jouy looks so much better when it is a little faded, while denim becomes more interesting after each wash. Linens bleach out in the same way, leaving only a hint of their original colour as a pale distant memory, while part of the essence of the traditional English interior is its well-worn, faded charm.

Subtle colours are also associated with fragility and delicacy. The palest pink cyclamen look utterly vulnerable on their fine stalks, while the soft baby-blue flowers of the climbing Cape leadwort (*Plumbago auriculata*) hang delicately in clusters, making a cool splash in a conservatory (sun room). A pink *Phalaenopsis* orchid is a confection of sugary loveliness.

Pale colours can either look pure and innocent or chic and sophisticated. Place pink roses against black and the result is urban chic, a combination favoured by Coco

Chanel, but place them against a billowing, white muslin curtain, and the look is feminine and natural. Miniature hybrid roses suitable for growing indoors come in a range of colours. Available as bushes or trained as miniature standards, most are derived from *Rosa chinensis* 'Minima', but they will probably be labelled simply as 'miniature roses' in garden centres.

Lavender (*Lavandula*) has the attributes of beautiful colouring as well as a heady, sleep-inducing fragrance. Indeed, the colour of the purple-mauve flowerheads is set off perfectly by the silvery grey foliage and stems. This beautiful plant recalls romantic cottage gardens and purple Provençal fields. Lavender is really a garden plant, but it is simply irresistible for a short time in a bright sunny position indoors on, perhaps, a country dresser.

Pale blue and pure white is another great colour combination, suggesting lazy summer days, blue skies and fluffy white clouds. Choose a container in a contrasting colour to the plant – perhaps a white pot for a mauve campanula – but one still in tune with the theme, and then add an appropriate top dressing. Shells or even tiny starfish would evoke the seaside. Pieces of pale, bleached wood added to a bowl of orchids would create a miniature version of their natural tropical rainforest habitat.

Opposite A collection of china, lovingly chosen and unified by the simplicity of form of each piece, provides a fitting backdrop for bowls of fragrant lavender.

Right The severe black containers prevent this extravagant grid of pink miniature roses looking overly feminine.

spring

Indoor bulbs can be a wonderful antidote to short days in spring when it is too chilly outdoors for many things to flower. The miracle of beauty emerging from an unprepossessing bulb planted months before is always a delight that lifts the spirits.

Each autumn, you can have great fun visiting a specialist bulb supplier and selecting bulbs in a variety of sizes and with wondrously complex shapes. Some have papery skins, tinged with purple, others are textured, but all have a mane of little roots. Choose firm, healthy ones, and just add water.

The resulting plants lend themselves to both traditional and modern interiors, depending on the container you choose. Let the flowers do the showing off and pick a

container that blends with the style of your interior. Bulbs do not need compost in the short term for nourishment, merely to stabilize them. By using transparent containers, almost filled with gravel or stones, you can watch the roots grow and easily judge the amount of water the plant needs. The bulb should be suspended above, but not touching, the water to prevent rotting.

Usually among the first flowers to break through the winter soil are crocuses with their pretty little vase-shaped flowers in yellow, white or purple. A large bowl of these would evoke a small garden, although they do not last for long in a warm environment. Plant the old bulbs outside after flowering. The intense deep purple of *Iris* 'George', with little else but its complex flowerhead showing above the planting medium, is strangely beautiful. Set the purple off against blue-grey slate chippings for maximum impact and use a silver or glass container.

The pure white flowers of heavily perfumed hyacinths (*Hyacinthus orientalis*) are perhaps the epitome of spring. They would create a strong sculptural effect in a fireplace in a modern apartment, top-dressed with white pebbles and with a layer of moss to hide the potting compost (soil mix). In contrast, the ethereal beauty of paper-white *Narcissus papyraceus* will work well in any style of home. The flowers also have the loveliest of scents. The stems often need supporting.

Left A simple basket is just the right container for these beautifully scented, paper-white narcissi (*Narcissus papyraceus*). The addition of woodland twigs is both functional and decorative.

summer

Summer is a time for flowers in the brightest colours and headiest scents, as well as of ripening fruits. It is also when hot sunshine shining through glass can damage plants, scorching the leaves and drying out the potting compost, so constant vigilance is important.

For a natural, informal feel indoors during the summer, plant a mass of colourful nasturtiums, which are easy to grow from seed, in a galvanized trough. Their round leaves set off the multicoloured flowers beautifully. The flowers are edible and make simple salads look pretty and summery.

Watery delights are very much a part of summer too. For an unusual display, float aquatic plants in a large glass bowl or tank. They do not need any compost, getting all their nutrients from the water. Water hyacinths (*Eichhornia crassipes*) have bulbous stems, rounded leaves and a delicate, short-lived flower. Water lettuce (*Pistia stratiotes*) has strongly ribbed leaves and would look starkly modern as a table decoration, the hair-like roots fanning out beneath the greenery for added interest.

Some plants are so beautiful that they take your breath away. The bird-of-paradise (*Strelitzia reginae*) is one such plant. It has blue-grey, lance-shaped leaves held high on rigid stems in a sculptural clump. The leaves are majestic, but the flowers are the most spectacular show of exotic, bird-like forms, with vibrant spathes and purple and orange flowers resembling a cabaret of plumed dancers. The flowers are sequential: when one plume dies down, another pops up. If the replacement fails to appear, just hook your finger inside the green 'beak' and help the new flower to emerge. They only flower when the plant has reached maturity at about six years old and do best in a conservatory (sun room).

Right These dark red pelargoniums are literally sunbathing in their metal containers.

Less demanding and equally beautiful is the arum or calla lily, *Zantedeschia aethiopica*. The classic variety has pure white spathes, but there are now many hybrids available in other colours, such as dark red or flecked with yellow. The leaves are sometimes spotted with translucent white flecks and are beautiful in their own right. Put a group in a large container to create the massed effect of their natural habitat.

autumn

This is the time when fruits and berries have ripened, the light is more golden and diffuse, and colours are more muted and neutral. Most gardens are past their best in the autumn and having some fresh greenery indoors is an added seasonal bonus.

Many flowering plants bought or grown in the summer will continue to flower well into the autumn if they are watered and fed properly. African violets (*Saintpaulia*), geraniums (*Pelargonium*) and *Streptocarpus* will all produce flowers until mid-autumn and beyond. If you have a balcony or patio, many outdoor bulbs can be grown in pots and then brought indoors when they are about to flower. The plants should be acclimatized first, raising the temperature gradually before bringing them into a warm room. Late summer and autumn bulbs, such as some

varieties of lily (*Lilium*) and the pineapple plant (*Eucomis autumnalis*), make for an unusual display, while the autumn crocus (*Colchicum autumnale*) is sold in mid- and late summer for autumn flowering.

Succulents make good year-round plants, so they are ideal for the autumn. Their soft, often silvery, colouring also gives them a suitable mellowness at this time of year. The elegant *Aloe ferox*, for example, has rust-red marginal teeth or spikes that suit the seasonal autumnal colours. Planted in multiple pots and then lined up the length of a dining table, they create an interesting sculptural effect.

The unusual kangaroo paw plant (*Anigozanthos flavidus*) can flower all year round in a conservatory (sun room), but the velvety flowerheads and the clump-like habit make a comforting arrangement for this time of year. The yellow-green to brownish-red flowers look rather like flickering flames. Planted in a burnished copper bowl and top-dressed with a grey pebble mulch, they make a cheerful display.

To match this time of plenty, grow ornamental cabbages and kales (*Brassica oleracea*), which come in a range of colours from deep dark purple to the milkiest of creams mixed with green. The ornamental varieties are not edible, so just enjoy them for their vibrant colouring and frilly ostentation. They produce their best colours as the temperature drops in autumn and winter and flourish best in the cold outdoors, so only bring them in for a short time.

Left The kangaroo paw plant (*Anigozanthos flavidus*), with its rich colouring and fascinatingly hairy flowers, makes an unusual display in a fireplace before the winter fires are lit.

winter

When the garden is largely dormant, indoor plants can bring colour to our homes. Centrally heated homes with chilly windowsills, and maybe a draughty hall, are disaster areas for all but the most stoical of plants, so choose the variety and position carefully.

Some houseplants, such as the ubiquitous spider plant and rubber plant, are creeping back into fashion as ironic statements. There are, however, other suitable foliage plants with sculptural qualities that perfectly complement modern furniture and current styles of architecture. The velvety green leaves of the Kris plant (*Alocasia sanderiana*) are balanced on the end of long, thin stems. The waxy, dark green, pointed leaves also have remarkable white veining. This plant needs to be grown in hot and humid, tropical conditions, but it is well worth a try, and is perfect for growing in a conservatory (sun room). If you do not have a conservatory, the splendid giant taro (*Alocasia macrorrhiza*) is an excellent alternative. The huge leaves are easily damaged, so make sure you give this plant plenty of space to appreciate its magnificent beauty. Remember its origins in swampy areas of South-east Asia, and keep it well watered and misted.

To have a tree growing indoors seems to be the ultimate triumph, a reversal of what is expected and a validation of your gardening abilities. *Ficus* 'Ali King', a large specimen of the fig genus, has a mass of long, dark green, glossy leaves and elegant, pendulous branches. It could be the only plant you need to refresh your spirits during a grey winter.

Early winter sees a plethora of seasonal pot plants, including the red poinsettia (*Euphorbia pulcherrima*). Green-and-white versions are easier to fit into a modern setting.

Above right Clipped box standards (*Buxus*) bring a touch of greenery indoors during a cold winter. They are really garden plants, but will be fine if they are brought indoors for just a few days.

There is a wealth of other brightly coloured plants that are available all through winter, including *Jasminum polyanthum*, azalea (*Rhododendron simsii*) and *Cyclamen persicum*. Hybrids of *C. persicum* are available in every shade of pink, red, white and purple, as well as bicolour combinations. For an unlimited colour choice, consider growing *Primula obconica*, which can have flowers in white, blue and apricot, as well as various shades of pink, crimson and scarlet. It is known commonly as the poison primrose because its leaves can cause dermatitis if handled by anyone allergic to it.

a lime-green garden

Green is a refreshing and invigorating colour. The leaves of the insect-eating plants used here need to be seen at close quarters if you are to fully appreciate the complexity of the shading. Placed in a conservatory (sun room), they will also help to control flying pests organically.

you will need

a large bowl, measuring about 50cm
    (20in) in diameter
drainage material, such as stones or
    pieces of pot
potting compost (soil mix):
    ⅔ peat substitute and ⅓ perlite
    or washed sand
3 pitcher plants (*Sarracenia*)
7 Venus flytraps (*Dionaea muscipula*)
small indoor gardening tools
rainwater or cooled boiled water

1 If you intend to make this a permanent display, ensure the bowl you use has drainage holes. You can create these using a ceramic drill if it doesn't have them. Put a layer of drainage material in the bottom of the bowl, then half fill it with potting compost.

2 Carefully take the plants from their plastic pots. Arrange the tall pitcher plants in the centre of the bowl and add more potting compost, to within 2cm (1in) of the rim of the bowl.

3 Plant the Venus flytraps around the edge of the bowl, scooping out shallow planting holes and spacing them out evenly. Gently firm in the potting compost with your fingers so that it is level and the plants are secure.

4 Water in the plants well, using rainwater or boiled water that has been allowed to cool down. Tap water is unsuitable for these plants. Position in an area with high humidity, such as a conservatory (sun room), and water regularly to keep the potting compost moist.

a scented white garden

This gloriously scented arrangement of pure white flowers combined with rich green, textural foliage will last far longer than a vase of cut flowers. The plants are simply placed in the decorative display container in their individual pots, and can be replaced at any time.

you will need

a large interesting container,
    in this case an antique leather
    water carrier
a sheet of heavy-duty plastic sheeting
a bucket of water
white gardenias (*Gardenia augusta*
    'Veitchiana'), white miniature
    roses (*Rosa*) and white jasmine
    (*Jasminum polyanthum*) in
    equal quantities
moss, if necessary

1 Loosely line the container with heavy-duty plastic sheeting in order to prevent water from damaging the container or the piece of furniture on which it will eventually be positioned.

2 Plunge the plants in their pots in a bucket of water until the bubbles stop and drain before arranging. Place the gardenias in their pots around the edge of the container, leaving room between each one for a potted rose.

3 Arrange the potted roses alternately between the gardenias. They should be snug, but not squashed.

4 Fill the central void with the jasmine and, if need be, add some moss between the plants to hide any gaps.

VARIATION You could change the feel of this display by using an assortment of your favourite plants. It makes sense to use one taller specimen in the centre, as this gives the arrangement a good shape.

a dry garden

For a contemporary space create a sculptural desert garden of agaves and cacti. The advantage of these plants is that they do not require constant watering or attention. In fact, a little neglect will do them no harm if you are away from home for a few weeks.

you will need

a boldly shaped container

drainage material, such as stones or
  pieces of pot

cactus potting compost (soil mix)

1 *Agave americana* 'Marginata'

1 *Agave stricta*

2 *Agave victoriae-reginae*

1 *Pachypodium lamerei*

a pair of gardening gloves

a watering can

grey stone chippings

1 Cover the bottom of the container with a layer of stones or broken pieces of terracotta pot, to a depth of about 8cm (3in). This is for drainage, as desert plants do not like being too wet.

2 Three-quarters fill the container with the cactus potting compost and arrange the plants carefully in position. Wear gloves when doing this because the spines will be very sharp.

3 Fill in any gaps with more potting compost, packing it in carefully to avoid creating air pockets.

4 Water the plants in well, using tepid water that has stood at room temperature for some time.

5 Cover the surface of the potting compost with a generous top dressing of grey stone chippings. Not only will this show off the architectural form of the plants, but it is also evocative of their natural environment.

a minimal garden

Create a contemplative garden of moss and gravel, using primeval-looking living stones (*Lithops*) as rocky outcrops. The simple black lacquer tray provides a graphic outline to the display. The moss will last a few months, but the living stones will probably outlast you.

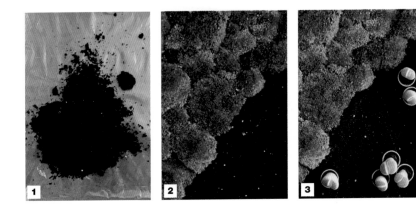

you will need

a sheet of heavy-duty plastic sheeting

a pair of scissors

a shallow container such as a black
    lacquer tray

cactus potting compost (soil mix)

1 basket of bun moss from a
    florist's shop

6 living stones (*Lithops*)

fine grit sold specifically for cactus
    displays

spray-mister

1 Cut a liner of heavy-duty plastic sheeting to fit exactly into the base and sides of a shallow container. Line the container with the sheeting, and cover with cactus potting compost.

2 Arrange the bun moss over half the area, using the best pieces to create little hills. Use the smaller pieces to fill in all the gaps around the edges. You should create a solid surface with no spaces.

3 Arrange the living stones in their tiny pots, moving them around until they look like ancient rocks in a Japanese monastery, then plant them in the potting compost once you are happy with their positions.

4 Water the plants in well, using tepid water that has stood at room temperature for some time.

5 Cover all the potting compost with a generous layer of the fine grit and mist the moss with a fine spray of filtered water or rainwater.

a summer meadow

Bring the pleasures of a wild-flower meadow into an urban setting with this display of lime-green wheatgrass and buttercup-yellow tickseed. Health-food stores sell wheatgrass or a growing kit – keep clipping the grass and add to the juicer for a healthy drink.

you will need

4 square metal containers or a
    large tray
drainage material, such as stones,
    gravel, broken pieces of old
    terracotta pot
a large tray of sprouted wheatgrass
    (*Elymus*)
2 trays of tickseed (*Coreopsis*)
a small bag of loam-based potting
    compost (soil mix)
a sharp carving knife
a watering can

1 Cover the bottom of each metal container with a good layer of drainage material. You will need to plant up two containers with wheatgrass and two with tickseed.

2 Add a layer of potting compost to the first container. Remove the sprouted wheatgrass from its tray, and, with a sharp knife, cut half of it to fit the container precisely. Repeat for the other container of wheatgrass.

3 Remove the tickseed plants from their plastic pots. Add a layer of potting compost to the two remaining metal containers. Pack the plants tightly into them. Add more potting compost, if necessary, to fill in any gaps.

4 Water in all the plants well. Position the plants neatly next to each other on a table. Here, a tray of wheatgrass is placed butting up to a container of tickseed, with the grass more or less concealing the join. The same is done with the other two, but the other way round, to create a pleasing asymmetry. This is not a long-lasting display, but then neither are some summers!

a tomato and basil garden

Classic Italian dishes are often based around the sublimely fragrant mix of tomatoes and basil. Using dwarf tomatoes and two different varieties of basil, you can grow your own simple appetizer indoors on a windowsill, which smells and tastes as good as it looks.

you will need

drainage material, such as stones,
  or pieces of pot
a long, narrow trough, about 20cm
  (8in) deep and 15cm (6in) wide
loam-based potting compost (soil mix)
4 dwarf tomato plants
  (*Lycopersicon esculentum*)
5 purple basil plants (*Ocimum
  basilicum* 'Purple Ruffles')
3 green basil plants (*Ocimum basilicum*)
a small trowel
a watering can
tomato fertilizer

1 Place a layer of drainage material in the bottom of a long, narrow trough and half-fill the container with a layer of loam-based potting compost.

2 Set out the tomato plants in their final planting positions. They should be spaced at 15cm (6in) intervals.

3 Place the purple basil in the gaps between the tomato plants at the front of the trough, and the green basil behind, to make an attractive display.

4 Fill in the gaps with more potting compost, firm in with your hands and water in well. Feed with a tomato fertilizer on a weekly basis and water daily.

5 When the tomatoes are ripe, slice them, sprinkle with freshly picked chopped green and purple basil, drizzle with extra virgin olive oil and eat.

VARIATION Instead of the purple basil, you could plant nasturtiums. They are not only attractive, but taste wonderful in salads.

plant
focus

In order to keep your plants in top condition it is important that you look after them properly. This section provides advice on basic techniques, such as potting, pruning and tackling pests and diseases, as well as a directory, which gives more detailed botanical information.

Left A row of sprouting daffodil and iris bulbs planted in alternately coloured pots make a beautiful display in spring.

caring for plants

Giving your plants the correct amount of light, food and water and the correct temperature and humidity is crucial to successful plant care. Isolating a plant in a pot means that it cannot search down for nutrients and water, as it would in the ground, while water will also drain away less quickly.

Light levels

Before buying a plant, think about where you will put it because light level requirements vary from plant to plant. Good garden centres and nurseries will advise you on your choice, which will help prevent expensive errors. Read the plant labels and follow the notes on care, particularly on light levels and watering.

Most flowering houseplants need good light levels, but will tolerate a less sunny position for a couple of weeks as long as they are moved back into the light afterward. Although artificial lighting can help boost light levels in dark spots indoors, it cannot compare with natural daylight. Most houseplants prefer bright, filtered, natural light. This means that they do not like to bake on sunny windowsills and need shade from hot midday sun.

In general, flowering plants need higher light levels than foliage plants, while plants with dark green leaves need less than those with silver-grey leaves. If there is too much light, the leaves will shrivel up and fall off or become bleached and pale. The potting compost (soil mix) will also dry out quickly in full sun and the plant's roots will be unable to penetrate the baked potting compost. A window that gets afternoon sun, rather than stronger midday sun, is usually a good place.

Plants that like to be moist are also usually shade-lovers. They are happy in a more humid room, such as a bathroom, with indirect light. But they still need light, so use pale-coloured walls to reflect light.

Temperature and humidity

Many houseplants prefer a daytime temperature of 18–21°C (64–70°F). In the directory, this is referred to as average warmth. Some plants require a cooler temperature during their dormant phase in late autumn and winter. Centrally heated homes can be too hot and dry for plants, with radiators below windowsills making this area hot during the day and often chilly and draughty at night.

Plants breathe through their leaves, but they also lose moisture through them, so raising the humidity around their pots can be beneficial for replacing this. A little water poured into a pebble-filled tray will raise humidity

Left Standing plants in a tray of damp, expanded clay granules will increase the humidity around them. Grouping plants together also raises humidity levels.

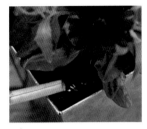   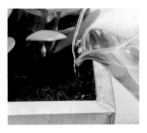

Above Top watering. **Above** Bottom watering. **Above** Watering a bromeliad. **Above** Adding liquid feed.

levels without the plant having to sit directly in the water and risk becoming waterlogged. Grouping plants together also raises the humidity around them.

Conservatories (sun rooms) need good ventilation. They should be fitted with windows that open, as well as some form of shading. Opening windows improves air circulation, but can also let in cold draughts. Finding the right balance is difficult, so invest in a device with a digital readout, showing inside and outside temperatures, as well as relative humidity. If the air is too humid, mould will appear on leaves and drought-loving plants will show patches of rot. Tell-tale signs of inadequate humidity levels are buds falling off or not opening, and leaves turning yellow and drooping or turning brown at the tips. Containers of rainwater will increase humidity. Hand-held misters can also be useful; mist twice a day in hot weather.

Watering

Spring and summer are the growing seasons for most plants. During this time, they need regular water to produce new shoots and flowers. They rest in autumn and winter and need less water, just enough to keep the potting compost from drying out. Overwatering is the commonest cause of death for many plants.

Many plants dislike hard tap water. Ideally, you should use rainwater, cooled boiled water or filtered water instead. When using tap water, always allow it to sit in the watering can until it has reached room temperature.

There are a number of different ways of watering:

Top watering Water from above using a long-spouted watering can, avoiding the leaves. Direct the spout at the compost.

Bottom watering Water from below, allowing the pot to sit in a tray of water until the compost has absorbed as much water as it can. Discard any surplus.

Plunging the pot Plunge the pot into a bucket of water until the compost is moist, but not waterlogged; then allow surplus water to drain away.

Bromeliad watering Some bromeliads hold water in a rosette of bracts which forms a cone-shaped cup. Carefully pour a little rainwater into this, topping up the cone when it is empty. Mist the plant regularly.

Feeding

Fresh potting compost has added nutrients, but, over time and after continued watering, these are used up, so potted plants need an occasional feed in the form of a balanced fertilizer. Liquid feeds are usually sold in concentrated form and need diluting carefully. Apply when the plant is in growth or flowering. A foliar feed applied to the leaves works as a quick pick-me-up, but move the plants outside . before spraying because the minerals can leave stains. Other ways of feeding include sprinkling slow-release granules into the potting compost when planting up or pushing a feeding stick into the compost. Always follow the manufacturer's instructions.

potting and pruning

Most plants bought at nurseries and garden centres come in small plastic pots with the roots already trying to escape through the bottom. At some stage after you buy them, they will need to be potted on into a larger pot with fresh potting compost.

Checking for diseases

Carefully examine all new plants before bringing them indoors. Gently ease the plant out of its pot and have a look to see whether there are signs of vine weevil, a pest that has become rampant in pots in recent years. The plant may show no sign of disease until it suddenly flops in the pot and a colony of white grubs with brown heads are found to have attacked the roots or bored into bulbs and rhizomes.

Potting composts

Choosing the right potting compost (soil mix) is vital to plant health. Garden soil is unsuitable, containing weed seeds as well as pests and diseases. There are two main types of potting compost: loam-based and soil-less. Sand or grit can be added to both of these to improve drainage.

Loam-based potting composts are more like garden soil, but are broken down into a fine mixture and sterilized. They usually contain added fertilizers and hold moisture well. Their weight will also help to hold the plant firmly in place and stabilize the pot. Soil-less potting composts are traditionally based on peat, but this is environmentally unfriendly, so choose peat-substitute ones. Both peat-based and peat-substitute composts tend to dry out easily and, once they have dried out, they are harder to rehydrate than loam-based types. The composts may have a numbering system to denote their suitability for different applications.

Certain plants need specialist growing mediums. Some orchids and bromeliads, for example, are epiphytic, which means they grow in trees. They feed on the rotting vegetable matter and bark that accumulates in the forks of trees, their roots in a loose compost that allows air to circulate around them. Specialist nurseries and good garden centres should be able to supply suitable composts. Cacti and succulents also do better in a special cactus potting compost, which is very free-draining.

Potting on

Plants can be traumatized by being potted on, but will recover most easily if it is done in spring.

1 Choose a clean container that is one or two sizes larger than the current pot. Fill the bottom with drainage material, covering but not blocking the drainage holes.

2 Cover with a layer of fresh potting compost (soil mix) and tap down. Position the plant about 2cm (¾in) below the rim of the pot to allow space for watering.

3 Spoon potting compost around the sides of the root ball and tap down. Continue until the compost is packed to leave a firm surface. Water in well.

Above Pinching out.

Above Dead-heading.

Above Cutting back.

Top-dressing

Mature plants may not need potting on, but will have exhausted their potting compost. Scrape off the top layer of old compost and replace with fresh compost. Water in well with a liquid fertilizer or add slow-release fertilizer.

Pinching out

You can encourage some plants to bush out by pinching out the leading shoots, resulting in new growth lower down. Tomato and pepper plants respond well in spring and summer.

Dead-heading

The act of picking off any flowers that are past their best, known as dead-heading, will encourage the plant to produce more. Their aim in life is to reproduce, so removing the flowerheads jolts them into producing more flowers (and so seed-heads). Indoor roses will last much longer if they are treated in this way.

Right Top-dress plants that do not need repotting, but have probably exhausted their old potting compost. Removing the top layer of old compost and providing a fresh new layer can be beneficial.

Cutting back

If a plant becomes too large, cut it back using a pair of secateurs (hand pruners). The weeping fig (*Ficus benjamina*) responds well to cutting back quite severely. This is best done at the end of the dormant period in late winter or early spring as it causes less shock. You can stop climbing plants, such as *Jasminum polyanthum*, becoming straggly by cutting back slightly after flowering and tying in wayward shoots to a framework of canes or wires.

problem-solving

Most problems associated with plants grown indoors are due to lighting levels, over- or underwatering, or incorrect temperatures. As a result plants may become stressed, making them more susceptible to pests and diseases, so it is important to keep an eye on them.

Common problems

Prevention is always better than cure, so be vigilant and spot signs of distress early on.

Upper leaves turn yellow Often the result of watering lime-hating plants with hard tap water. Use cooled boiled or filtered water, or rainwater. Try using a proprietary feed formulated for acid-loving plants.

Flower-buds dropping off or not opening Caused by insufficient light and/or humidity, or lack of water.

Brown spots and patches on leaves Could be caused by too much sunlight scorching the leaves, by drops of water on sensitive leaves or insects. Move the plant out of strong sunlight and inspect the underside of the leaves. If insects are discovered, try brushing or rubbing them off, or use an insecticide if the infestation is severe.

Leaves curling at edges and dropping off Possibly caused by the plant being in a cold draught, or by overwatering. Some insects can also have this effect.

Leaves with brown tips and/or edges The result of lack of humidity or being in too hot a window. Can also be caused by tap water, which contains chemicals,

Left Carefully remove leaves with brown edges or tips or which have died altogether with secateurs or small scissors.

so try using rainwater or filtered water, or cooled boiled water. Remove the leaves because they will not recover.

Wilting leaves A sign of either underwatering or overwatering. May also be caused by vine weevil, which feed on roots. If you find a bad infestation, throw away the whole plant immediately.

Sudden leaf fall Single leaves fall off all the time, but if all the leaves fall off, then the plant has had a shock – either extreme cold or heat or complete dehydration. The weeping fig (*Ficus benjamina*) is prone to this.

Rotting leaves or stems A sign of overwatering and poor drainage which encourages the mould to grow. Remove affected parts and spray with carbendazim.

Yellow patches between veins of leaves Can be caused by magnesium deficiency, which is easily treated by a dose of diluted Epsom salts (20g/¾oz per 1 litre/1¾ pints water) and with a foliar feed. Follow the manufacturer's instructions.

Pests

There are many different types of pests that can afflict indoor plants, but here is a list of some of the most common, and advice on how to deal with them. Always read manufacturers' labels and follow the instructions, and wherever possible, take plants outside to be treated. Keep all substances well away from children and animals.

Aphids Tiny green or black sap-sucking insects that cluster round leaf stems and tips. They leave behind a sticky substance, sometimes known as honeydew, which can become infected with black sooty mould. A strong jet of water may remove enough to limit the damage, if done regularly.

Otherwise, you can spray with an insecticidal soap, or a chemical control. Pirimicarb is an aphid-specific one. Aphids may spread viruses and weaken plants, but rarely kill them.
Red Spider Mite You will need a magnifying glass to see this mite and its white eggs on the underside of leaves, which may have a yellow mottling. There may also be a fine silky webbing. It causes the leaves to dry up and fall off until only shoot tips remain. Despite its name, the mite is yellowish-green, only becoming orange-red in autumn and winter. To treat, spray with insecticidal soap or a chemical control. Dispose of badly affected plants carefully. Spraying under leaves with water and keeping humidity high will discourage the pests.
Vine Weevil The adult is a brownish-grey beetle that bites semicircles into the edges of leaves. If you are not squeamish, pick them off and crush them. They are easier to spot in the evening as they tend to hide during the day. The unseen danger is the fat white grubs or larvae that are found at the bottom of the pot and which feed on the roots, causing sudden wilt and death. If this happens, dispose of the plant and surrounding compost immediately. One control of the larvae is available as microscopic pathogenic nematodes, *Steinernema kraussei* or *Heterorhabditis megidis*, which can be obtained from suppliers by post, and watered into the compost in late summer. The larvae are quite resistant to chemical controls.
Whitefly Clouds of very small, white winged insects, these reproduce very quickly and are becoming resistant to insecticides. The adults and their whitish-green, scale-like nymphs feed on sap from the undersides of the leaves, which weakens the plant, and the sticky honeydew they secrete encourages the growth of moulds. One quite effective way of trapping them is by positioning sticky yellow sheets around the affected plants. Small parasitic wasps, *Encarsia formosa*, are available by mail order, but these are not a suitable option where the conservatory (sun room) is an integral part of the living space. You can spray with an insecticidal soap or a chemical insecticide.

Right Check the leaves of plants regularly. Using a magnifying glass will enable you to spot even very small pests or their eggs.
Below right This camellia is infested with aphids that can, if left untreated, damage the plant.

Diseases
A disease is usually the symptoms caused by a small parasite that attacks a plant's cells. They are usually caused by fungi, bacteria or viruses, and by the time symptoms become obvious, they may have already caused substantial damage. Keeping everything spotlessly clean will help to prevent problems occurring, so tidy up dead leaves and flowers and ensure pots are clean.
Grey mould This greyish white fuzzy growth on leaves and stems is caused by the fungus *Botrytis cinerea* and is prevalent in very humid conditions. The airborne spores only usually infect healthy plants via cuts or tears. It thrives in dead matter and can remain dormant in plant tissue for months. Improve the circulation of air around the plants and remove badly affected plants immediately.
Anthracnose Causing leaves to turn yellow then dark brown and eventually die, this disease is caused by the fungi *Colletrotrichum* and *Gloeosporium*, which enter the plant via wounds. Destroy any affected leaves and avoid misting the plant.
Powdery mildew The formation of a white, powdery growth or dry, brown, papery leaf spots is caused by the fungus *Oidium* species. Improve air circulation and avoid overwatering, and remove any affected leaves.

containers

Choosing suitable, attractive pots is vitally important. A collection of square, round and rectangular containers in different materials is a great starting point. Plain ones suit both urban and rural interiors and will not detract from the impact of the plant.

Shape and texture

Build up a collection of simple graphic shapes in materials such as glass, metal and stone in various sizes. Long, low containers look wonderful on a mantelpiece or hall table, while softer, more rounded containers might be more suitable for a bedside table. Perspex (Plexiglas) or glass ones are good for seeing the roots of spring bulbs. Different materials create different moods. Concrete and metal look urban and edgy, terracotta and ceramic more rustic. Baskets lined with plastic sheeting have a more traditional feel and look good with spring or autumnal arrangements.

Rough-textured pots in materials such as concrete look wonderful with succulent plants, and suggest the sort of dry landscape from which these specimens originate. With

glass containers, place the potted plant inside and fill the spaces with pebbles or slate chippings, moss or gravel – in fact, anything small and interesting that will give an extra design dimension.

Style and form

Both the container and arrangement should relate to the design of the room. Strong angular furniture in a modern, loft-style apartment needs strong architectural displays to reinforce the design, whereas soft and sensual planting in a romantic

bedroom makes for a relaxing atmosphere. Kitchens are where many people socialize, so including a few plants is a must. The kitchen should also offer up a wealth of containers, including bowls, stainless-steel pans and buckets. If there are no drainage holes, use a deep layer of gravel or other drainage material in the base and take extra care when watering.

With many people now working from home, there is often a study or home office where plants can play a role. Containers should be crisp and business-like here, or perhaps add a splash of colour to an otherwise monochrome scheme. When working on computer screens, it is advisable to rest your eyes for a few moments every twenty minutes or so. What better to rest them on than a beautiful plant or group of plants?

Shopping tips

Buying pots can be as much fun as searching for plants. Old farm pails and bins are currently in favour in smart florists' shops, while chicken feeders can be used as window boxes. Auction sales can be a source of original containers, and many delightful pieces can be found, cleaned and polished, and then added to the appropriate interior.

Some pots come with their own matching water tray, but standing a pot within a decorative container usually looks better. It is important to check regularly that water is not building up in the base, as this could lead to mildew.

Left Old terracotta pots have an enduring appeal and are perfect for collections of herbs and bulbs.

tools and accessories

Once the pleasures of indoor gardening have taken hold, you will need an assortment of tools and accessories to help you keep the arrangements in pristine condition. Using the smartest implements, you will soon find that tending your plants is as rewarding as admiring them.

Gardening gloves and tools

One of the most important items in your indoor gardening toolkit is a pair of gardening gloves, especially for handling prickly cacti. It is possible to find long-handled, miniature versions of garden trowels and forks to make digging around in a small pot easier. Of course, it is just as good to use old kitchen spoons and forks, but not nearly so stylish.

Watering cans and misters

A can with a long spout is useful for reaching between leaves and directing the water to where you want it to be rather than bouncing off the leaves on to your precious furniture. There are so many well-designed modern watering cans available that they are just too good to put away. A fine pump-action mister is also useful because moisture is absorbed through the leaves of plants and it also helps to keep dust from dulling them.

Stakes, supports and labels

Your plants may need support as they grow. Canes and stakes are strong and practical but don't always look good. So, collect interesting branches on walks (sometimes with the added bonus of lichen) and use these. Birch twigs pushed into the potting compost (soil mix) in a container both support fragile stems and enhance a composition. Colourful chopsticks can also make elegant supports for smaller plants, while reeds soaked in water can be used to

Right A ball of string and some beech plant labels are both decorative and useful.

make horizontal supports between canes. Sometimes string or wire is needed to anchor the wayward stems of vigorous plants. A collection of plant labels in different materials, such as slate and wood, is also invaluable, making the process of identifying your plants so much more enjoyable than with ugly plastic labels.

Drainage material

Never throw away broken terracotta pots; just break them up into small pieces to use as crocks for drainage at the bottom of another pot. Try to keep everything spotlessly clean both to prevent cross infection of bugs and viruses and because it looks so much more attractive. If you are lucky enough to have a special area for all your indoor-gardening tasks, so much the better.

Mulches and top dressings

Experiment with decorative mulches and top dressings. They can be stored in other pots or glass jars for easy access, and will add a finishing touch to your plant arrangements. A top dressing of moss would suit a more traditional display in a terracotta pot, but there are also other more modern mulches, including buttons, shells, fossils, pebbles, stones, coloured gravel, crushed glass, metal-coated pellets and even dried starfish.

directory of indoor plants

Begonia
Begonia

The leaves of *B. rex* hybrids are variegated in shades of green, silver, brown, red, pink and purple. The leaves of *B.* 'Norah Bedson' are blotched brown and green.

Light Bright/indirect.

Temperature Cool.

Watering and feeding Water freely and apply a liquid fertilizer at every second watering when in growth. Water sparingly in winter.

Cultivation Repot in spring in a loam-based potting compost (soil mix).

Blechnum gibbum
Hard fern

This is an evergreen fern with tall, lance-shaped fronds that uncurl

beautifully from the centre. It can also be grown successfully in the garden.

Light Bright/indirect.

Temperature Cool.

Watering and feeding Keep moist. Mist regularly or stand in a tray of damp gravel. Apply a high-nitrogen liquid fertilizer at half strength occasionally when in growth.

Cultivation Pot on in spring, using a loam-based potting compost with added bark, charcoal and sharp sand.

Capsicum annuum **Longum Group**
Chilli pepper

The conical ornamental peppers are held upright on bushy plants. The fruits turn from green to purple to red.

Light Bright/indirect.

Temperature Warm; humid.

Watering and feeding Water freely when in growth and sparingly in winter. Apply a balanced liquid fertilizer every two weeks when in growth until the fruits start to colour.

Cultivation Grow in loam-based potting compost.

Clerodendrum myricoides **'Ugandense'**
Blue glory bower

This evergreen climber from West Africa is best grown in a conservatory (sun room). It has blue to purple flowers with long lower 'lips'. The winding stems can be trained around a hoop. *C. thomsoniae* can be grown indoors, but also prefers a conservatory.

It has dark green, heart-shaped leaves and red and white flowers in summer.

Light Bright/indirect.

Temperature Warm.

Watering and feeding Water freely and apply a balanced liquid fertilizer monthly when in growth. Water sparingly in winter.

Cultivation When pot-bound, pot on in loam-based potting compost. Dead-head regularly to produce more flowers.

Crocus vernus
Dutch crocus

Some cultivars of Dutch crocus have bold, funnel-shaped flowers in white, blue or purple. When grown outdoors, they usually open like a goblet, but in the

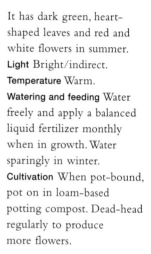

Begonia 'Norah Bedson'

Blechnum gibbum

Capsicum annuum Longum Group

Clerodendrum myricoides 'Ugandense'

Crocus vernus

Cyclamen persicum

Cyperus involucratus

Ficus carica

warmth of a conservatory (sun room) or on a sunny windowsill they open fully.
Light Bright/indirect.
Temperature Cool.
Watering and feeding Keep moist when dormant, water freely when in growth. There is no need to feed.
Cultivation Plant corms in loam-based compost in autumn and keep in a cool, dark place until the leaves emerge, then bring into the light.

Cyclamen
Cyclamen
It is the florists' cyclamen derived from *C. persicum* that is usually grown indoors. It is available in a range of sizes and colours. The petals may be frilled or ruffled. The leaves are often marbled with white or silver. They can flower from autumn to early spring.

Light Bright/indirect.
Temperature Cool to warm.
Watering and feeding Water freely when in growth, reducing the amount after flowering. Keep dry during the resting period. Feed every two weeks when growing and flowering.
Cultivation Grow in a loam-based potting compost, enriched with leaf mould and added grit. Keep dry when dormant, repot in autumn and water to restart growth.

Cyperus involucratus
Umbrella plant
This clump-forming plant, which looks like a collection of umbrellas, grows in water in the wild, but it can be grown as a houseplant if it is given enough moisture. Small, yellowish-white flowers appear in summer.
Light Bright/indirect.
Temperature Cool.

Watering and feeding Keep waterlogged at all times. Stand the pot in a shallow tray of water; a piece of charcoal will keep the water 'sweet'. Apply a balanced liquid fertilizer monthly when in growth.
Cultivation In spring, divide overcrowded plants and pot up in a loam-based potting compost, top-dressed with gravel.

Ficus
Fig
The figs used as houseplants are grown for their foliage. The common fig (*F. carica*) can grow up to 2.1m (7ft) in the home, but a younger plant looks spectacular displayed on a plinth. *F.* 'Ali King' is an evergreen that enjoys being indoors. The long, shiny, elliptical leaves are held on slender elegant branches. The weeping fig

(*F. benjamina*) can grow to 1.5m (5ft) given the right conditions and is one of the most effective plants for purifying the air. The creeping fig (*F. pumila*) is an evergreen, trailing climber that looks good growing underneath larger specimens. Figs may lose their leaves if shocked by draughts, lack of water or being moved.
Light Bright/filtered.
Temperature Average.
Watering and feeding Water freely when in growth (large plants will need frequent watering as the larger area of the leaves loses water faster). Feed monthly with a high-nitrogen liquid fertilizer when in growth. Figs respond well to generous feeding.
Cultivation When pot-bound, pot on using a loam-based compost with added bark.

Gardenia augusta 'Veitchiana'

Guzmania lingulata

Hyacinthus orientalis

Iris 'George'

Gardenia augusta 'Veitchiana'

The shiny leaves contrast beautifully with the white, fragrant short-lived flowers.
Light Bright/indirect.
Temperature Cool to average.
Watering and feeding Water freely and apply a balanced liquid fertilizer monthly when in growth. Water sparingly in winter. Use soft or demineralized water and never let the roots dry out.
Cultivation Repot in spring, using an ericaceous potting compost (soil mix).

Guzmania lingulata

These exotic bromeliads, mainly from the tropical rainforests of South America, are usually grown for their showy bracts. Dark green, lance-shaped leaves form a funnel that holds water. The flower stalk is topped by bright red or orange bracts that wrap around tiny, yellowish-white flowers.
Light Bright/filtered.
Temperature Very warm; humid. Provide cooler conditions in winter.
Watering and feeding When in growth, water moderately with rainwater or filtered water, filling the centres. Water sparingly in winter. No feeding is required.
Cultivation Grow in bromeliad potting compost. Guzmanias rarely need repotting.

Hyacinthus orientalis
Hyacinth

The pink, blue or white flowers are strongly scented. Use specially prepared bulbs for forcing indoors; plant in a cool, dark place and bring into the light when shoots emerge. Keep cool until they flower.
Light Bright/indirect.
Temperature Cool.
Watering and feeding Water moderately when in growth.
Cultivation Grow in peat-substitute potting compost. Discard or plant outside.

Impatiens hybrids
Busy Lizzie

Masses of flat flowers appear at any time of the year if the temperature is maintained above 16°C (60°F). Blooms are mostly in shades of red, orange, pink and white, of which many are multi-coloured and sometimes double. The flowers of the New Guinea Group are usually fewer but larger.
Light Bright/indirect.
Temperature Cool to average; humid.
Watering and feeding Water freely and feed every two weeks when in growth. Water sparingly in winter.

Cultivation Repot in spring if necessary. They are easy to grow, so raise new plants from cuttings and discard if they become leggy.

Iris
Iris

The irises grown as short-term indoor plants are dwarf bulbous species, including yellow-flowered I. danfordiae and I. reticulata, which has blue or purple flowers, depending on the variety. I. 'George' has dramatic, deep purple flowers from late winter to early spring.
Light Bright/filtered.
Temperature Cool.
Watering and feeding Keep the potting compost moist.
Cultivation Plant bulbs in early or mid-autumn, then place outside. When shoots appear, bring indoors and keep in a light place. Discard or replant outside.

Lavandula
Lavender
Aromatic evergreen shrubs with grey-green leaves and mauve, pink or white flowers. They are garden plants, but can be brought inside for a while or overwintered in a conservatory (sun room). *L. angustifolia* 'Munstead' has spikes of purple-blue flowers.
Light Bright/filtered.
Temperature Cool to warm.
Watering and feeding Water moderately and apply a balanced liquid fertilizer monthly when in growth. Water sparingly in winter.
Cultivation Grow in a loam-based potting compost with added grit or perlite.

Lilium hybrids
Lily
The bulbs in this genus that are grown as pot plants are usually hybrids. They have become popular indoor plants with the introduction of compact varieties. Most hybrids have trumpet-shaped or backward curving petals in shades of red, orange, yellow and white, usually spotted, mottled, or flushed with another colour. 'Casa Blanca' is a striking white variety.
Light Bright/filtered.
Temperature Cool to average.
Watering and feeding Water freely and apply a high-potash liquid fertilizer every few weeks when in growth.
Cultivation Bulbs are usually planted in a loam-based compost in autumn or mid- to late winter, depending on when they are available. Keep the bulbs in a cool, dry place, with the compost just moist. When the buds show colour, move to a warmer room, but avoid high temperatures, which will shorten the life of the blooms. Plant outside after flowering.

Lithops
Living stone, stone plant
These intriguing, dwarf, stemless succulents from southern Africa look like greenish-brown stones with a smooth surface. The pairs of fused, swollen leaves grow into small clumps. The pairs of leaves part to produce a single flower in late summer. Many species are available, but you are most likely to find *L. bella*, which has brownish-yellow, fused leaves with depressed, darker patches. White, daisy-like flowers appear in late summer or early autumn. Planted in a shallow tray that is top-dressed with gravel and small stones, it is difficult to distinguish the real stones from the living ones.
Light Bright/filtered.
Temperature Warm, dry, average room.
Watering and feeding Water with great care, only moderately in summer and not at all in winter. Start watering again when the new leaves appear. Feeding is seldom necessary, but if the plant has been in the same pot for many years, feed occasionally with a cactus fertilizer.
Cultivation Grow in cactus potting compost with added leaf mould and good drainage.

Narcissus
Daffodil
Daffodils herald the arrival of spring. *N.* 'Tête-à-Tête' is a dwarf daffodil with golden yellow flowers. It can be planted in a basket for a traditional look or in a clear container for a modern feel. The paper-white narcissus (*N. papyraceus*) has strongly scented white flowers. 'Ziva' is suitable for forcing.

Lavandula angustifolia 'Munstead'

Lilium hybrid

Lithops

Narcissus 'Tête-à-Tête'

Light Bright/indirect.
Temperature Cool.
Watering and feeding Water moderately when in growth. Continue watering if replanting outside.
Cultivation Plant new bulbs in autumn in a loam-based potting compost (soil mix) in a cool dark place. When shoots appear, bring into a warmer room.

Paphiopedilum hybrids
Slipper orchid
These winter-flowering evergreen orchids make attractive houseplants. *P. parishii* has twisted, brown-spotted, greenish petals, which are pendulous, and a greenish-brown pouch.
Light Partial shade.
Temperature Cool to average; likes humidity.
Watering and feeding Water freely and apply an orchid fertilizer every three to four weeks when in growth. Mist daily. Water sparingly in winter.
Cultivation Enjoys being pot-bound, but, if potting on, use a terrestrial orchid potting compost.

Pelargonium
Pelargonium
Grown for their colourful flowers or scented leaves, pelargoniums are ideal for a sunny windowsill or conservatory (sun room). There are different groups in a range of colours, including Regal (single flowers in single or combined shades of red, pink, purple, orange, white or reddish black); Ivy-leaved (single to double flowers in shades of red, pink, mauve, purple or white); and Zonal (single or double flowers in shades of scarlet, purple, pink, white, orange and rarely yellow). As well as their showy flowers, pelargoniums have attractive leaves; large, bold and round or small and ivy-shaped. The Scented-leaved pelargoniums have small, single flowers in shades of mauve, pink, purple or white, and are largely grown for the strong aromas that are released when you brush against the leaves. Scented species include *P. capitatum* and *P. graveolens* (rose-scented); *P. crispum* (lemon-scented); and *P. tomentosum* (peppermint-scented).
Light Bright/filtered.
Temperature Warm.
Watering and feeding Water moderately, applying a liquid fertilizer every two weeks when in growth. Water sparingly in winter.
Cultivation Pot on in loam-based or peat-substitute potting compost. Cut back in late winter/early spring. Dead-head for more flowers.

Phalaenopsis hybrids
Moth orchid
These evergreen orchids are ideal for a warm home. The stems of flowers will last for months, and may appear more than once a year.
Light Bright/indirect; no direct sun.
Temperature Warm; humid.
Watering and feeding Water freely when in growth and sparingly in winter. Mist daily. Apply an orchid fertilizer monthly when in growth.
Cultivation Grow in a transparent pot using epiphytic orchid potting compost. Likes to be pot-bound.

Plumbago auriculata
Cape leadwort
This evergreen conservatory (sun room) climber from South Africa has clusters of pale blue flowers. There is a white variety, *P. a.* var. *alba*.

Paphiopedilum parishii

Pelargonium Ivy-leaved Group

Phalaenopsis 'Paifang's Golden Lion'

Plumbago auriculata var. *alba*

Primula obconica

Soleirolia soleirolii

Strelitzia reginae

Tacca chantrieri

Light Bright/filtered.
Temperature Cool to warm.
Watering and feeding Water freely when in growth and sparingly in winter. Apply a balanced liquid fertilizer every two weeks in spring and summer.
Cultivation Pot on in the spring, using a loam-based potting compost.

Primula obconica
Poison primrose
The pale green leaves may cause an allergic reaction. Pink, white or blue flowers appear in winter and spring.
Light Bright/indirect.
Temperature Cool.
Watering and feeding Water freely when in growth and sparingly in winter. Apply a half-strength liquid fertilizer once a week when in flower.
Cultivation Pot on in loam-based potting compost with added grit or perlite.

Soleirolia soleirolii
Mind-your-own-business
This spreading plant is used as ground cover in gardens, but forms mounds of green foliage if grown in a pot indoors. The tiny leaves are held on thin stems that give the plant a fragile look. It likes damp conditions.
Light Bright/indirect.
Temperature Cool to warm; humid.
Watering and feeding Water freely and apply a liquid fertilizer monthly when in growth. Water sparingly in winter. Mist regularly.
Cultivation In late spring, divide the plant and pot on in a loam-based potting compost.

Strelitzia reginae
Bird of paradise
Resembling an exotic bird of paradise, the long-lasting, orange and blue flowers sit

in a boat-like bract. Only the species can be grown as an indoor plant. The main flowering period is spring.
Light Bright/filtered.
Temperature Warm.
Watering and feeding Water freely and apply a balanced liquid fertilizer monthly when in growth. Water sparingly in winter.
Cultivation Divide and plant root suckers in a loam-based potting compost in spring.

Tacca chantrieri
Bat flower, devil flower
Weird and beautiful, the flower of this perennial has green, bell-shaped petals surrounded by pairs of darker green, or black, floral bracts and hung with long 'whiskers', thread-like appendages that can reach up to 25cm (10in) in length.
Light Partial shade.
Temperature Warm; humid.

Watering and feeding Water freely throughout the year. In summer, mist regularly and apply a half-strength foliar feed monthly.
Cultivation Pot on every few years, using equal parts coarse bark and leaf mould, with added slow-release fertilizer.

Yucca
Yucca
Two species are grown as indoor plants. The leaves of *Y. aloifolia* grow in a dense rosette and have sharp points. *Y. elephantipes* is similar, but the leaf tips are not sharp.
Light Bright/filtered.
Temperature Cool.
Watering and feeding Water freely when in growth and sparingly in winter. Apply a balanced liquid fertilizer monthly in summer.
Cultivation Repot small plants in loam-based compost. Top-dress large plants.

index

1	21	41	61	81	101	121	141	161	181
2	22	42	62	82	102	122	142	162	182
3	23	43	63	83	103	123	143	163	183
4	24	44	64	84	104	124	144	164	184
5	25	45	65	85	105	125	145	165	185
6	26	46	66	86	106	126	146	166	186
7	27	47	67	87	107	127	147	167	187
8	28	48	68	88	108	128	148	168	188
9	29	49	69	89	109	129	149	169	189
10	30	50	70	90	110	130	150	170	190
11	31	51	71	91	111	131	151	171	191
12	32	52	72	92	112	132	152	172	192
13	33	53	73	93	113	133	153	173	193
14	34	54	74	94	114	134	154	174	194
15	35	55	75	95	115	135	155	175	195
16	36	56	76	96	116	136	156	176	196
17	37	57	77	97	117	137	157	177	197
18	38	58	78	98	118	138	158	178	198
19	39	59	79	99	119	139	159	179	199
20	40	60	80	100	120	140	160	180	200

201	216	231	246	261	276	291	306	321	336
202	217	232	247	262	277	292	307	(322)	337
203	218	233	248	263	278	293	308	323	338
204	219	234	249	264	279	294	309	324	339
205	220	235	250	265	280	295	310	325	340
206	221	236	251	266	281	296	311	326	341
207	222	237	252	267	282	297	312	327	342
208	223	238	253	268	283	298	313	328	343
209	224	239	254	269	284	299	314	329	344
210	225	240	255	270	285	300	315	330	345
211	226	241	256	271	286	301	316	331	346
212	227	242	257	272	287	302	317	332	347
213	228	243	258	273	288	303	318	333	348
214	229	244	259	274	289	304	319	334	349
215	230	245	260	275	290	305	320	335	350